CHARLOTTE'S WEB

Written by E.B. White

Student Study Guide

MEMORIA PRESS
www.MemoriaPress.com

CHARLOTTE'S WEB
Written by E.B. White

STUDENT STUDY GUIDE
Contributing Editors: Leigh Lowe, Brenda Janke, Anne Parry, Brittany Mann

ISBN 978-1-61538-047-3

Cover illustration by Starr Steinbach

Contents

Charlotte's Web

Appendix 67

PREPARING TO READ:

REVIEW

- Orally review any previous vocabulary.
- Review the plot of the book as read so far.
- Periodically review the concepts of character, setting, and plot.

STUDY GUIDE PREVIEW

- Reading Notes:
    - Read aloud together
    - This section gives the student key characters, places, terms that are relevant to a particular time period, etc.
- Vocabulary:
    - Read aloud together so that students will recognize words when they come across them in their reading.
- Comprehension Questions:
    - Read through these questions with students to encourage purposeful reading.

READING:

- Student reads the chapter (or selection of the chapter for that lesson) independently or to the teacher (for younger students).
- For younger students, you can alternate between teacher-read and student-read passages. Model good reading skills. Encourage students to read expressively and smoothly. Teacher may occasionally take oral reading grades.
- While reading, mark each vocabulary word as you come across it.
- Have students take note in their study guide margin of pages where a comprehension question is answered.

AFTER READING:

VOCABULARY

- Look at each word within the context that it is used, and help your student come up with the best synonym that defines the word. (Make sure it is a synonym the student knows the meaning of.)
- Record the word's meaning in the students' study guides. (Use students' knowledge of Latin and other vocabulary to decipher meanings.)

COMPREHENSION QUESTIONS

- Older students can answer these questions independently, but younger students (2nd-4th) need to answer the questions orally, form a good sentence, and then write it down, using correct punctuation, capitalization, and spelling. (You may want to write the sentence down for the younger student after forming it orally, and then let the student copy it perfectly.)
- It is not necessary to write the answer to every question. Some may be better answered orally.
- Answering questions and composing answers is a valuable learning activity. Questions require students to think; writing a concise answer is a good composition exercise.

QUOTATIONS AND DISCUSSION QUESTIONS

- Use the Quotations and Discussion Questions section of each lesson as a guide to your oral discussion of the key concepts in the chapter that may not be covered in the comprehension questions.
- These talking points can take your oral discussion to a higher level than covered in the students' written work. Use this time as an opportunity to introduce higher-level thinking. You can introduce concepts the students may not be mature enough to fully understand yet but that would be beneficial for them to begin thinking about.
- A key to the Discussion Questions is in the back of the Teacher Guide.

ENRICHMENT

- The Enrichment activities include composition, copywork, dictation, research, mapping, drawing, poetry work, literary terms, and more.
  - This section has a variety of activities in it, but the most valuable activity is composition. Your student should complete at least one composition assignment each week. Proof student's work and have student copy composition until grammatically perfect. Insist on clear, concise writing. For younger students, start with 2-3 sentences, and do the assignment together. The student can form good sentences orally as you write them down, and then the student copies them.
- These activities can be completed as time and interest allow. Do not feel you need to complete all of these activities. Choose the ones that you feel are the best use of your students' time.

UNIT REVIEW AND TESTS

- There is a unit review and a quiz or test following every few lessons (varies by individual guide).
- On the weeks that have these reviews and tests, you may want to do the review early in the week, and then drill it orally a couple of times before giving the test at the end of the week.
- A final comprehensive test is also included.

Reading Notes

plaster a paste applied to walls which hardens as it dries

roller towel a long, continuous towel sewed together and hung on a roller; it can be washed and reused

dagger a short sword-like weapon

specimen an example

Vocabulary

1. one of the pigs is a **runt**. ______
2. I know more about raising a **litter** of pigs than you do. ______
3. This is the most terrible case of **injustice** I ever heard of. ______
4. Saved from an **untimely** death. ______
5. No, I only **distribute** pigs to early risers. ______

Comprehension Questions

1. Name each Arable family member, including the children's ages. Fern was 8. Mrs. Arable. and Mr. Arable. Avery was 10.
2. How does Fern convince her father not to kill the runt? What is her reasoning? She said "If I had been very small at birth, would you have killed me?"
3. What is the first thing Fern teaches her pig? She teaches her pig to eat.
4. What does Fern name her pig? Why does she choose that name? She name her pig Wilbur. it was the most beautful name she
5. Why does Fern say "Wilbur" instead of answering her teacher's questions about Pennsylvania's capital? She was thinking of Wilbur.

Quotations

"But it's unfair," cried Fern. "The pig couldn't help being born small, could it? If I *had been very small at birth, would you have killed* me*?" Mr. Arable smiled. "Certainly not," he said, looking down at his daughter with love. "But this is different. A little girl is one thing, a little runty pig is another."*

Fern couldn't take her eyes off the tiny pig. "Oh," she whispered. "Oh, look *at him! He's absolutely perfect."*

Discussion Questions

1. *What does the word "arable" mean? From what Latin word does "arable" come? Why is it a good name for a farm family?
2. Study the pictures on pages 5 and 6. How has the illustrator contrasted Avery and Fern?
3. Reread Fern's objection to the runt's death and Mr. Arable's reply in the first quote above. In what way is a pig different than a little girl? Who do you agree with, and why?

   * Discussion questions that have a * are NECESSARY to discuss with students, as they may appear on a test and are generally important in understanding the full flavor of the story.

Enrichment

Focus Passage: Copy the 2nd and 3rd paragraphs from page 5 (beginning with "Can I have a pig …" and ending with "Let's eat!").

What is Mr. Arable subtly trying to communicate to Avery through his response?

Reading Notes

apple-blossom time	springtime
enchanted	fascinated
manure	animal excrement
cellar	a room beneath the barn

Vocabulary

1. He would stand and **gaze** up at her with adoring eyes. ______
2. Fern **peered** through the door. ______
3. It **relieved** her mind to know that her baby would sleep covered up______
4. he would stand and watch the bus until it **vanished** around a turn. ______
5. When she **waded** into the brook, Wilbur waded in with her. ______

Comprehension Questions

1. How does Wilbur keep himself warm on cold nights? he dug a tunnel in the straw.

2. Describe some of the ways Fern pampers Wilbur. She whold put wilbur in the doll carriaga.

3. How does Fern feel about Wilbur? How does Wilbur feel about Fern? Fern loves wilber and wilber loves fFern.

4. Who buys Wilbur? For how much? he was sold to the Zuckermans for six dollars.

Quotations

Fern loved Wilbur more than anything. She loved to stroke him, to feed him, to put him to bed. Every morning, as soon as she got up, she warmed his milk, tied his bib on, and held the bottle for him....Wilbur loved his milk, and he was never happier than when Fern was warming up a bottle for him. He would stand and gaze up at her with adoring eyes.

"He's got to go, Fern," he said. "You have had your fun raising a baby pig, but Wilbur is not a baby any longer and he has got to be sold."

Who said this? ______________________________

Discussion Questions

1. Since straw is not a main source of food, what is it used for on a farm?
2. Why is Fern's father able to predict what Wilbur will do to stay warm in his wooden box?
3. Why does Wilbur enjoy playing in the mud that is "delightfully sticky and oozy"?
4. *What reasons does Father give for insisting that Fern sell Wilbur?

Enrichment

Order and Describe: List Wilbur's first three homes in their correct order. Then, below each one, list vivid words that describe it.

1.____________________	2.____________________	3. ____________________
______________	______________	______________
______________	______________	______________
______________	______________	______________
______________	______________	______________
______________	______________	______________
______________	______________	______________
______________	______________	______________
______________	______________	______________

Reading Notes

grindstones, pitch forks, monkey wrenches, scythes	tools used for sharpening, adjusting, and cutting
rooting	to dig up
slops	watery food
hullabaloo	a clamorous noise

Vocabulary

1. It smelled of the **perspiration** of tired horses ______
2. The cocker spaniel heard the **commotion** ______
3. He's trying to **lure** you back into captivity-ivity. ______
4. He's trying to lure you back into **captivity**-ivity. ______
5. He's **appealing** to your stomach. ______

Comprehension Questions

1. What is a sheepfold? Why do you think the geese live with the sheep? ______

______

______

______

2. Who is the first animal Wilbur meets? How does she influence him? ______

______

______

3. Why does Wilbur so willingly follow the advice of the goose at first? ______

______

______

4. What is Wilbur's final opinion of his freedom and eventual recapture? ______

______

______

______

Quotations

The barn was very large. It was very old. It smelled of hay and it smelled of manure. It smelled of the perspiration of tired horses and the wonderful sweet breath of patient cows. It often had a sort of peaceful smell—as though nothing bad could happen ever again in the world.

"I'm really too young to go out into the world alone," he thought as he lay down.

Who said this? ______________________ On what occasion? ______________________

Discussion Questions

1. Describe the barn; how it looks, what it contains, and how it feels.
2. *List the animals living in the barn. Describe the homes of each.
3. *Explain the goose's warning: "He's appealing to your stomach."
4. What causes Wilbur to change his mind about being free? What does he long for?

Enrichment

Focus Passage: Copy the first full paragraph on page 14 (beginning with "Wilbur's new home …"). Spelling, punctuation, and capitalization should be perfect.

____

____

____

____

____

____

____

____

____

____

____

Reading Notes

hominy	dried corn
provender	hay or oats used for livestock feed
flibbertigibbet	a silly, scatterbrained person

Vocabulary

1. I am a **glutton** but not a merrymaker. ______
2. And Templeton, the rat, crept **stealthily** along the wall ______
3. Usually he … was **abroad** only after dark. ______
4. **dejected** and hungry, he threw himself down in the manure ______
5. He didn't know whether he could **endure** the awful loneliness______

Comprehension Questions

1. Describe the appearance, personality, and attitude of Templeton.______

______

______

2. What does Wilbur do to try to cure his loneliness? ______

______

______

3. How do the goose, Templeton, and the lamb react to Wilbur's request? ______

______

______

4. Why does Wilbur declare the day the "worst of his life"? ______

______

______

5. What is Wilbur's pleasant surprise at the end of the day? ______

______

______

Quotations

Wilbur didn't want food, he wanted love. He wanted a friend—someone who would play with him.

"I prefer to spend my time eating, gnawing, spying, and hiding. I am a glutton but not a merrymaker."

Who said this? ______________________ To whom? ______________________

Discussion Questions

1. *Which of the illustrations in Chapter 4 shows Wilbur at his saddest? How can you tell?
2. Who says, "Pigs mean less than nothing to me"? How does Wilbur respond to this statement?
3. In the second quote above, what does Templeton mean by "I am a glutton but not a merrymaker"?
4. What does Lurvy do to try to make Wilbur feel better? Why?

Enrichment

Composition: Wilbur experienced a very disappointing and lonely day. He was not able to accomplish any of his plans for the day. Have you ever had a day like Wilbur's?

Directions: Write a paragraph (3-5 sentences) explaining your day. Use the following questions to guide your composition: What were your plans? How did they change? How did you feel? (Don't forget to indent your paragraph!)

Reading Notes

Charlotte *A. Cavatica*	a reference to a barn spider's scientific name, *Araneaus cavaticus*
inheritance	a genetic characteristic passed from parent to offspring
"by my wits"	by cleverness

Vocabulary

1. I didn't mean to be **objectionable**. ______
2. He lay down **meekly** in the manure ______
3. A fly … **blundered** into the lower part of Charlotte's web ______
4. and although he **detested** flies, he was sorry for this one. ______
5. Wilbur was **merely** suffering the doubts and fears ______

Comprehension Questions

1. What word does Charlotte use to greet Wilbur? What Latin root means "greetings"? What is the opening of a friendly letter called? ______
2. How does the author describe Charlotte? How does Charlotte describe herself? ______
3. What does Charlotte do for a "living"? How does she capture prey? ______
4. How does Charlotte defend herself and convince Wilbur that webs are a good thing? ______

Quotations

"Well," he thought, "I've got a new friend, all right. But what a gamble friendship is!"

Who said this? ______________________ On what occasion? ______________________

Wilbur was merely suffering the doubts and fears that often go with finding a new friend. In good time he was to discover that he was mistaken about Charlotte. Underneath her rather bold and cruel exterior, she had a kind heart, and she was to prove loyal and true to the very end.

Discussion Questions

1. Before Charlotte greets him, Wilbur is impatient, embarrassed, and humble. Describe how Wilbur demonstrates these qualities toward the beginning of the chapter.
2. Describe in detail Charlotte's process for obtaining food.
3. Contrast how Charlotte obtains her food compared to how Wilbur receives his. What does this say about Charlotte?
4. *Explain Wilbur's statement, "… what a gamble friendship is!" in the first quote above.

Enrichment

Dialogue is back-and-forth conversational exchange. Each time a new character begins speaking, there is a new set of quotation marks, and a new paragraph begins with indentation.

Directions: Copy the dialogue between Charlotte and Wilbur from page 37 (beginning with "'My name,' said the spider …" and ending with "… as clearly as you can see me." Spelling, punctuation, and capitalization should be perfect.

____

____

____

____

____

____

____

____

Reading Notes

swathes	long, narrow rows of cut grass or grain
jubilee	celebration
Fridgidaire	a brand of refrigerator
dud	a failure

Vocabulary

1. Then the hay would be **hoisted** ______
2. Sweet, sweet, sweet **interlude** ______
3. after four weeks of **unremitting** effort and patience ______
4. The rat had no morals … no **scruples** … no anything. ______
5. The rat had no morals … no **compunctions** … no anything. ______
6. He pushed … till he succeeded in rolling it to his **lair**. ______

Comprehension Questions

1. Describe early summer days on the farm. ______
2. Where is Fern in this chapter? How do the animals treat her? ______
3. What is the important event that happens in the barn cellar? Who announces it? ______
4. Where does Templeton put the "dud" goose egg? ______

Quotations

The rat had no morals, no conscience, no scruples, no consideration, no decency, no milk of rodent kindness, no compunctions, no higher feeling, no friendliness, no anything. He would kill a gosling if he could get away with it—the goose knew that. Everybody knew it.

"But, my friends, if that ancient egg ever breaks, this barn will be untenable."

What does "untenable" mean? ______________________

Discussion Questions

1. List four birds mentioned in the chapter. Describe each bird's song.
2. Explain the statement, "A rotten egg is a regular stink bomb."

Enrichment

Characterization: Using what you know about Templeton from this chapter and previous ones, fill in the characterization chart below. Use specific examples from the book and include the page number of where the example was found.

Ways Templeton's character is revealed	Example	What you learn about Templeton from this example
Templeton's speech		
Templeton's appearance		
How other characters feel about Templeton and react to him		
Templeton's actions		

Reading Notes

victim someone who is harmed by another
anaesthetic pain killer
conspiracy secret plan to do harm

Vocabulary

1. Her **campaign** against insects seemed sensible and useful. ______________________
2. Her campaign against insects seemed **sensible** and useful. ______________________
3. Flies spent their time **pestering** others. ______________________
4. The sheep **loathed** them. ______________________
5. I can't stand **hysterics**. ______________________

Comprehension Questions

1. What does Charlotte do that Wilbur describes as "real thoughtful"? ______________________

____

____

2. What bad news is spreading in the barnyard? Who passes it on to Wilbur? ______________________

____

____

3. Contrast Wilbur's and Charlotte's reactions to the bad news. ______________________

____

____

____

4. What promise does Charlotte make? ______________________

____

5. What does Charlotte tell Wilbur to do? Why? ______________________

____

____

Quotations

Wilbur liked Charlotte better and better each day. Her campaign against insects seemed sensible and useful.

Wilbur burst into tears. "I don't ***want*** *to die," he moaned. "I want to stay alive, right here in my comfortable manure pile with all my friends. I want to breathe the beautiful air and lie in the beautiful sun."*

Discussion Questions

1. *Think about the first quote above and the first few paragraphs of the chapter. How has Wilbur's opinion of Charlotte's activities changed?
2. *Reread the second quote above. How has Wilbur's outlook on life been altered since his earlier days on the farm?

Enrichment

Quotation Review: How good is your memory? Supply the name of the speaker for each quotation below.

1. "But it's unfair … The pig couldn't help being born small, could it?" ______________
2. "I only distribute pigs to early risers." ______________
3. "Get around behind him, Lurvy … and drive him toward the barn!" ______________
4. "No-no-no … It's the old pail trick, Wilbur. Don't fall for it!" ______________
5. "Pigs mean less than nothing to me." ______________
6. "I am a glutton but not a merrymaker." ______________
7. "I'll be a friend to you. I've watched you all day and I like you." ______________
8. "… they're fattening you up because they're going to kill you …" ______________
9. "Stop! … I don't want to die! Save me, somebody!" ______________
10. "… Stop your crying! I can't stand hysterics." ______________

Elements of Literature

Write sentences about the story.

Character

Character means <u>who</u> is in the story.

1. Write one declarative sentence describing Wilbur. Include his age and personality. ____________

____

2. Write one interrogative sentence (question) about another character in the story. Include words that describe this character's appearance and personality. ____________________

____

Setting

Setting means the <u>time</u> and <u>place</u> in which the story happens.

1. Write one exclamatory sentence about the Arable farm. ____________________

____

2. Write one descriptive sentence about Mr. Zuckerman's barn. Be sure to include strong imagery (sights, sounds, smells) in your sentence. ____________________

____

Plot

Plot means <u>action</u> or <u>what happens</u> in the story.

Directions: Sequence the events in order. Then, copy them in order onto the following page. Each event should be written below a separate box. Finally, illustrate each event in the box.

Events:

_____ Charlotte became Wilbur's friend.

_____ Wilbur escaped from his pen.

_____ Wilbur learned he would be killed at Christmastime.

_____ Fern saved and cared for Wilbur.

_____ Templeton requested the rotten goose egg.

_____ Wilbur was lonely and bored.

Vocabulary

Write the letter of the vocabulary word on the line in front of its definition.

1. _______ smallest of the litter	a. blundered
2. _______ unfairness	b. injustice
3. _______ to deliver; give out	c. commotion
4. _______ to look at steadily	d. meekly
5. _______ disappeared	e. waded
6. _______ walked in shallow water	f. endure
7. _______ state of being held against your will	g. hysterics
8. _______ noisy, confused activity	h. runt
9. _______ to attract through other means	i. loathed
10. _______ one who habitually overeats	j. vanished
11. _______ to bear, tolerate	k. dejected
12. _______ disappointed; discouraged	l. merely
13. _______ humbly	m. distribute
14. _______ only; simply	n. hoisted
15. _______ moved carelessly	o. captivity
16. _______ lifted; pulled up by a device	p. lair
17. _______ den	q. glutton
18. _______ constant; neverending	r. unremitting
19. _______ exaggerated, uncontrolled emotions	s. gaze
20. _______ strongly disliked	t. appealing

Short Answer

Answer the following questions in complete sentences.

1. What does the word "arable" mean? Why is it a good name for a farm family? ______

2. What reasons does Father give for insisting that Fern sell Wilbur? ______

3. What important event, announced by Charlotte, happens in the barn cellar? ______

4. Explain Wilbur's statement, "… what a gamble friendship is!" ______

5. What promise does Charlotte make to Wilbur? ______

Reading Notes

goslings (pronounced "goz-lings") baby geese

Sunday School a class for religious instruction that meets on Sundays

Vocabulary

1. gazing at her daughter with a **queer**, worried look. ____________________
2. She's **terribly** clever. ____________________
3. "Does he really?" said Mrs. Arable, rather **vaguely**. ____________________
4. I haven't the **faintest** idea, ____________________
5. every one of us … will be **gratified** to learn ____________________
6. Did you hear the way she **rambled** on about the animals …? ____________________

Comprehension Questions

1. Why is Mrs. Arable worried about Fern? ____________________
2. How does Mr. Arable respond to Mrs. Arable's concern? ____________________
3. What does Mrs. Arable plan to do to ease her mind about Fern? ____________________
4. Fern often sits quietly on a stool in the barn. After reading this chapter, what do you now know she has been doing while in the barn? ____________________

Quotations

"She's Wilbur's best friend. She's terribly clever."

Who said this? ______________________ To whom? ______________________

Mr. Arable grinned. "Maybe our ears aren't as sharp as Fern's," he said.

Discussion Questions

1. What is your opinion about talking animals?

Enrichment

Focus Passage: Copy the third and fourth full paragraphs from page 54 (beginning with "I worry about Fern …" and ending with "… all sorts of things.")

Notice: There are two separate paragraphs that need to be indented. Be careful to copy all quotation marks accurately. Spelling, punctuation, and capitalization should be perfect.

Reading Notes

hitches	easily loosened knots that attach a rope to an object
sedentary	accustomed to sitting or to taking little exercise
truffles	edible fungi; grow near the roots of trees
troupe	a group of musicians

Vocabulary

1. He glanced **hastily** behind to see if a piece of rope was following him ____________________
2. Anything to **oblige**. ____________________
3. And **summoning** all his strength, he threw himself into the air ____________________
4. In a forest looking for … **delectable** roots ____________________
5. But don't fail to let me know … no matter how **slight**. ____________________

Comprehension Questions

1. List the sections of Charlotte's legs. What interesting attributes do her legs have? ____________________

   ____

   ____

   ____

2. How does Wilbur try to imitate Charlotte? Why does he fail? ____________________

   ____

3. In what ways does Charlotte think her webs are better than human "webs" (i.e., bridges)? ____________________

   ____

   ____

   ____

   ____

4. What instructions does Charlotte give Wilbur to help carry out "the plan"? ____________________

   ____

   ____

Quotations

While the rat and the spider and the little girl watched, Wilbur climbed again to the top of the manure pile, full of energy and hope.

"I want you to get plenty of sleep, and stop worrying. Never hurry and never worry! Chew your food thoroughly and eat every bit of it, except you must leave just enough for Templeton. Gain weight and stay well—that's the way you can help."

Who said this? ______________________________ To whom? ______________________________

Discussion Questions

1. In this chapter, Wilbur tries several times to accomplish something that he was not made to do. How can we discover our own unique gifts and talents? How can we encourage our friends and family to do the same?
2. What observations does Charlotte make about people in this chapter? Do you think she is correct in her assumptions?

Enrichment

Studying Details: Using the diagram of a spider in the Appendix as a reference, draw a detailed diagram of Charlotte below.

Label the seven parts of her legs and her spinnerets.

Complete your diagram by coloring it.

Reading Notes

crisis a terrible event
gabbled to speak rapidly and in a way that is difficult to understand
astride to sit or stand with one leg on each side of an object

Vocabulary

1. people are very **gullible**. ______
2. Then you **straddled** the knot, so that it acted as a seat. ______
3. Templeton … **scuttled** away into the barn. ______
4. "It pays to save things," he said in his **surly** voice. ______
5. After a while she **bestirred** herself. ______
6. She worked slowly … while the other creatures **drowsed**. ______

Comprehension Questions

1. On what attribute does Charlotte rely to help her solve problems? Give examples. ______
2. What idea comes to Charlotte to save Wilbur's life? Why does she think it will work? ______
3. What event stirs the barn animals and prevents a catastrophe? What catastrophe is prevented?
4. At the end of the chapter, why does Wilbur leave a whole noodle instead of half a noodle for Templeton? ______

Quotations

"Why, how perfectly simple!" she said to herself. "The way to save Wilbur's life is to play a trick on Zuckerman. If I can fool a bug," thought Charlotte, "I can surely fool a man. People are not as smart as bugs."

The spider, however, stayed wide awake, gazing affectionately at him and making plans for his future. Summer was half gone. She knew she didn't have much time.

Discussion Questions

1. Reread the second quote above. Has Wilbur done anything to earn or deserve Charlotte's affection? What does that say about the nature of friendship?
2. In what ways are Templeton, the goose, and Lurvy "accidental" heroes?
3. Describe the highlights of Fern's and Avery's day at the Zuckerman farm.

Enrichment

Dictation: Listen carefully as your teacher reads to you from page 72 (beginning with "Fern was crying …" through "… a narrow escape."). During the reading, write down what you hear. Then go back and make any necessary corrections in spelling, punctuation, or capitalization. When you are finished, compare your paragraph to the book and circle any errors.

Reading Notes

spang	directly
Studebaker, Packard, De Soto	types of cars; now antiques
buckboard	a four-wheeled wagon drawn by a horse or other large animal

Vocabulary

1. Charlotte, sleepy after her night's **exertions**, smiled ____________________
2. Instead, he walked **solemnly** back up to the house ____________________
3. A look of complete **bewilderment** came over Mrs. Zuckerman's face. ____________________
4. She's a rather queer child—full of **notions**. ____________________
5. his **principal** farm duty was to feed the pig ____________________

Comprehension Questions

1. Describe the beauty of the web. Who was the first person to discover it? ____________________

2. Charlotte's plan is finally unveiled. Describe it, and explain how it helps Wilbur. ____________________

3. How does Mrs. Zuckerman's view of the miracle differ from everyone else's? ____________________

4. What are specific ways the web affects life on the Zuckerman farm? ____________________

Quotations

Secrets are hard to keep. Long before Sunday came, the news spread all over the county. Everybody knew that a sign had appeared in a spider's web on the Zuckerman place. Everybody knew that the Zuckermans had a wondrous pig.

Mr. Zuckerman ordered Lurvy to increase Wilbur's feedings from three meals a day to four meals a day.

Discussion Questions

1. In the previous chapter, Charlotte said that humans are gullible. Give examples of specific ways from this chapter that prove Charlotte was correct in her observation.
2. Why do the Zuckermans and Lurvy change their personal appearance and habits once Wilbur becomes famous?

Enrichment

Character Study: Match each character to his or her reaction to Charlotte's web.

Lurvy	Mr. Zuckerman	townspeople	Fern
minister	Mrs. Arable	Mrs. Zuckerman	

1. ____________________ "But we have received a sign … a miracle has happened on this farm."
2. ____________________ "… this community has been visited by a wondrous animal."
3. ____________________ was so shocked that she sent Avery to bed for punishment
4. ____________________ "It seems to me we have no ordinary *spider."*
5. ____________________ dropped to his knees and uttered a short prayer
6. ____________________ was happy but felt the barn was not nearly as pleasant
7. ____________________ came to stand hour after hour at Wilbur's pen, admiring him

Reading Notes

St. Vitus's Dance	a disorder characterized by jerky, uncontrollable movements
baser instincts	needs or behaviors vital for survival

Vocabulary

1. It's my idio-idio-**idiosyncrasy**. ______
2. Any suggestions for a new **slogan**? ______
3. Wilbur's **destiny** and your **destiny** are closely linked. ______
4. Templeton's whiskers **quivered**. ______
5. The meeting is now **adjourned**. ______

Comprehension Questions

1. What does Charlotte want to discuss at the meeting? Who attends? ______
2. What role does the old sheep suggest Templeton could play in the plan to save Wilbur? ______
3. Why is Charlotte worried about Templeton's involvement? ______
4. What argument does the old sheep use to get Templeton to agree to help? ______

Quotations

"The message I wrote in my web, praising Wilbur, has been received. The Zuckermans have fallen for it, and so has everybody else. Zuckerman thinks Wilbur is an unusual pig, and therefore he won't want to kill him and eat him. I dare say my trick will work and Wilbur's life can be saved."

Who said this? ______________________ On what occasion? ______________________

"You're terrific as far as I'm *concerned," replied Charlotte, sweetly, "and that's what counts. You're my best friend, and* I *think you're sensational."*

Discussion Questions

1. Reread the first quote above. Why is Charlotte so confident that her plan to save Wilbur will work?
2. *What is Wilbur's reaction to the new word? What does this show about his character?
3. Why are some words italicized in the last two paragraphs of the chapter?

Enrichment

Focus Passage: Copy the second quote above. Pay close attention to quotation marks. (Ignore the italics.) Spelling, punctuation, and capitalization should be perfect.

Reading Notes

orb a sphere or spherical object
radial moving from the center to the outside of a circle (spokes)
aeronaut a pilot or traveler in a hot air balloon

Vocabulary

1. Templeton was down there now, **rummaging** around. ______
2. "There!" he said, **triumphantly**. ______
3. With New **Radiant** Action. ______
4. Wilbur went over backwards, **writhing** and twisting as he went. ______
5. Tired from his **romp**, Wilbur lay down ______

Comprehension Questions

1. Describe the types of thread Charlotte can produce. How is each used? ______
2. How does Charlotte entertain herself while weaving? ______
3. How do the words in Charlotte's web continue to affect how Wilbur is treated? ______
4. What two things does Charlotte do to help Wilbur go to sleep? How does this show her affectionate friendship toward Wilbur? ______

Quotations

Everybody stood at the pigpen and stared at the web and read the word, over and over, while Wilbur, who really felt *terrific, stood quietly swelling out his chest and swinging his snout from side to side.*

"Just the wrong idea," replied Charlotte. "Couldn't be worse. We don't want Zuckerman to think Wilbur is crunchy. He might start thinking about crisp, crunchy bacon and tasty ham. That would put ideas into his head. We must advertise Wilbur's noble qualities, not his tastiness. Go get another word, please, Templeton!"

Discussion Questions

1. List some of the things Templeton finds in the dump.
2. Describe some of the amazing qualities and abilities of Charlotte's relatives.

Enrichment

Italics are used to indicate titles of newspapers, books, or magazines. When copying italics, underline the words that are italicized. Italics can also be used to show emphasis. (Example: "… while Wilbur, who really *felt* terrific …")

Directions: Reread the first full paragraph on page 96 (beginning with "Terrific!" breathed …") Then copy it below. Pay close attention to the italicized title of the newspaper, and underline it in your paragraph. Spelling, punctuation, and capitalization should be perfect.

Reading Notes

fib	small lie; to tell a small lie
crochet	needlework made by looping thread using a hooked needle
doily	a small decorative mat made of thread

Vocabulary

1. "Fern," said her mother **sternly**, "you must not invent things." ____________________
2. she was beaten **mercilessly** over the head by the … fish ____________________
3. and is carried **aloft** on the wind. ____________________
4. It is a very **sociable** place. ____________________
5. an animal has spoken **civilly** to me ____________________
6. People are **incessant** talkers ____________________

Comprehension Questions

1. Why is Mrs. Arable alarmed by her conversation with Fern? ____________________
2. Describe Dr. Dorian. ____________________
3. How old is Fern? What does Dr. Dorian think about Fern's love of animals and spending so much time in the barn? ____________________
4. What observations does Dr. Dorian make about people? What is his opinion about spider webs? ____________________
5. What does Dr. Dorian suggest will, in time, get Fern's attention? ____________________

Quotations

"Alone?" said Fern. "Alone? My best friends are in the barn cellar. It is a very sociable place. Not at all lonely."

"It is quite possible that an animal has spoken civilly to me and that I didn't catch the remark because I wasn't paying attention. Children pay better attention than grownups. If Fern says that the animals in Zuckerman's barn talk, I'm quite ready to believe her. Perhaps if people talked less, animals would talk more. People are incessant talkers—I can give you my word on that."

Who said this? ______________________________ To whom? ______________________________

Discussion Questions

1. *Refer to the second quote above. How does Dr. Dorian explain the difference between the "miracle" of a spider web and the fact that Mrs. Arable can crochet a doily and knit a sock?
2. Contrast Mrs. Arable's and Dr. Dorian's attitudes about things they do not understand. Is there something you don't like because you don't understand it? How could you change your opinion?

Enrichment

Dialogue: Recall that **dialogue** is back-and-forth conversational exchange, and that **quotation marks** are used to show a person's exact words.

Directions: Insert quotation marks where they are needed in the following sentences.

1. Charlotte is the best storyteller I ever heard, said Fern.
2. What kind of story did she tell? asked Mrs. Arable.
3. Well, began Fern, she told us about her cousin who caught a fish in her web.
4. Fern! snapped her mother. Stop it! Stop inventing these wild tales!
5. I'm not inventing, said Fern. I'm just telling you the facts.
6. It's about Fern, she explained. Fern spends entirely too much time in the Zuckermans' barn.
7. How enchanting! he said. It must be real nice and quiet down there.
8. I suppose so, said Mrs. Arable. I never looked at it that way before. Still, I don't understand it.
9. None of us do, said Dr. Dorian, sighing. I don't understand everything, and I don't let it worry me.
10. Well, said Dr. Dorian, I think she will always love animals.

Reading Notes

reputation the characteristics or traits a person is known for
twitch a short, sudden pull or tug

Vocabulary

1. the song of summer's ending, a sad, **monotonous** song. ______
2. Wilbur was **modest**; fame did not spoil him. ______
3. If he could **distinguish** himself at the Fair______
4. "Oh, sure," said the spider. "I'm **versatile**." ______
5. Charlotte … **moodily** watched it sway. ______

Comprehension Questions

1. How does Wilbur try to live up to his reputation? ______
2. How has Charlotte influenced Wilbur's attitude towards life? ______
3. What does Wilbur do to act out the word "radiant"?______
4. What are Wilbur and Charlotte each looking forward to? How do these clash? ______
5. Why can't Charlotte delay her egg laying until after the fair?______

Quotations

Some of Wilbur's friends in the barn worried for fear all this attention would go to his head and make him stuck up. But it never did. Wilbur was modest; fame did not spoil him.

In the daytime, Wilbur usually felt happy and confident. No pig ever had truer friends, and he realized that friendship is one of the most satisfying things in the world.

Discussion Questions

1. ***A Lesson in Friendship:** Reread the second quote above. Describe how the following characters showed true friendship to Wilbur: Charlotte, Fern, the goose, the old sheep.
2. Describe some of the changes the farm experiences as the transition from summer to autumn begins.
3. How does the book hint at some future event concerning Charlotte? Does it sound exciting or unpleasant?

Enrichment

Focus Passage: Copy the second paragraph on page 114 (beginning with "The sheep heard the crickets ..." through "... bright red with anxiety."). Spelling, punctuation, and capitalization should be perfect.

Elements of Literature

Write sentences about the story.

Character

Character means <u>who</u> is in the story.

1. Write one declarative sentence describing Charlotte. ______________________________

____

2. Write a declarative sentence about another character in the story. Include words that describe this character's appearance and personality. ______________________________

____

Setting

Setting means the <u>time</u> and <u>place</u> in which the story happens.

1. Write two sentences describing the change of seasons in Chapter 15. ______________

____

____

____

____

Plot

Plot means <u>action</u> or <u>what happens</u> in the story.

Directions: Sequence the events in order. Then, copy them in order onto the following page. Each event should be written below a separate box. Finally, illustrate each event in the box.

Events:

_____ A "miracle" occurs in the barn.

_____ Two new webs are spun.

_____ Wilbur tries unsuccessfully to spin a web.

_____ The animals hold a meeting.

_____ Dr. Dorian gives Fern's mother good advice.

_____ A rotten goose egg saves Charlotte's life.

Vocabulary

Write the letter of the vocabulary word on the line in front of its definition.

1. _______ seriously; firmly		a. gullible
2. _______ pleased; satisfied		b. sociable
3. _______ unchanging		c. principal
4. _______ without clear thought		d. delectable
5. _______ into the air		e. quivered
6. _______ main; primary		f. bestirred
7. _______ physical efforts; work		g. writhing
8. _______ trembled		h. vaguely
9. _______ friendly		i. aloft
10. _______ squirming		j. summoning
11. _______ gathering; calling up		k. modest
12. _______ delicious; tasty		l. gratified
13. _______ humble		m. romp
14. _______ endless; continuous		n. versatile
15. _______ lively play; frolicking		o. adjourned
16. _______ easily deceived		p. incessant
17. _______ roused; moved		q. surly
18. _______ adaptable; can adjust easily		r. monotonous
19. _______ unfriendly; bad-tempered		s. exertions
20. _______ officially ended		t. sternly

Short Answer

Answer the following questions in complete sentences.

1. What plan does Charlotte come up with to save Wilbur's life? Why does she think it will work? ____

2. Name two specific ways in which the webs affect life on the Zuckerman farm. ____

3. What is Wilbur's reaction to the second word in the web ("terrific")? What does this show about his character? ____

4. As summer comes to an end, what are Wilbur and Charlotte each looking forward to? ____

5. Choose one of the following characters and describe how he/she shows friendship towards Wilbur: Charlotte, Fern, the goose, the old sheep. ____

Reading Notes

midway the area of a fair where the food, rides, and games are located
loot stolen goods
yarn an entertaining tale
stowaway a secret traveler
tailgate a door at the back of a vehicle that is lowered during loading and unloading

Vocabulary

1. you will find a **veritable** treasure of popcorn fragments ____________________
2. the conditions at a fair will **surpass** your wildest dreams. ____________________
3. Don't go without a **tussle**. ____________________
4. I don't want to be **pummeled** … **buffeted** … **biffed** ____________________
5. I don't want to be … **lacerated** ____________________

Comprehension Questions

1. What does Fern wear to the fair? Why? ____________________

____

2. What special treatment does Wilbur get before departing for the fair? ____________________

____

3. Why does Charlotte finally decide to go with Wilbur to the fair? ____________________

____

____

4. Why does the old sheep want to tempt Templeton to go to the fair? What delicious items does he tell the rat he will find? ____________________

____

____

5. What advice does the old sheep give Wilbur before he is crated for the fair? Why? ____________________

____

____

Quotations

"That's some pig!" said Mrs. Arable. "He's terrific," said Lurvy. "He's very radiant," said Fern, remembering the day he was born. "Well," said Mrs. Zuckerman, "he's clean, anyway. The buttermilk certainly helped."

Then, using all their strength, the men picked up the crate and heaved it aboard the truck. They did not know that under the straw was a rat, and inside a knothole was a big grey spider. They saw only a pig.

Discussion Questions

1. Describe the dreams of Fern, Avery, Mr. and Mrs. Zuckerman, and Lurvy the night before the fair.
2. *Reread the first quote above. How do the words in the web continue to influence people's thinking about Wilbur?
3. Authors often use repetition to emphasize a point in a story. In what way does the author use repetition in this chapter to make the story more interesting?

Enrichment

Literary Tools - Description: A good author uses descriptive words to paint a verbal picture for the reader.

Directions: Reread the last paragraph on page 122 (beginning with "That's because you've …" through "… a whole army of rats.").

A. Find, record, and discuss two or three descriptive phrases used by the author.

____

____

____

B. Add your own descriptive words to these examples from the paragraph.

hard-boiled eggs: ____

cracker crumbs: ____

popsicles: ____

C. Think of another item Templeton may have found at the fair. Write your own descriptive phrase, being sure to paint a vivid mental picture for the reader.

____

Reading Notes

blatting bleating
deep freeze a large freezer that resembles a chest

Vocabulary

1. She **ascended** slowly and returned to Wilbur's pen. ______
2. She looked rather swollen and she seemed **listless**. ______
3. "Perhaps," she said, **wearily**. ______
4. Wilbur heard several people make **favorable** remarks ______
5. The day grew **fiercely** hot. ______

Comprehension Questions

1. Describe the sights, sounds, and smells of the fair. ______
2. What privileges do Mr. and Mrs. Arable grant Fern and Avery at the fair? ______
3. Name Wilbur's main competitor. Why does Charlotte dislike him? ______
4. What changes does Charlotte begin to notice in herself while at the fair? ______

Quotations

The children grabbed each other by the hand and danced off in the direction of the merry-go-round, toward the wonderful music and the wonderful adventure and the wonderful excitement, into the wonderful midway where there would be no parents to guard them and guide them and where they could be happy and free and do as they pleased.

Charlotte, watching her chance, scrambled out of the crate and climbed a post to the under side of the roof. Nobody noticed her.

Discussion Questions

1. *Reread the second quote above, focusing on the last sentence. Why do you think Charlotte doesn't want to be noticed? What does she prefer?
2. *What signs are there of Wilbur becoming a better friend towards Charlotte?
3. Think back to the dreams in the beginning of Chapter 16. Did any of them come true in this chapter? Predict the outcome of Mr. Zuckerman's dream.

Enrichment

Focus Passage - Dialogue: Recall that **dialogue** is used to show a character's exact words. Each time a different character begins to speak, a new paragraph is begun and indented.

Directions: Copy the paragraphs of dialogue on page 131 (beginning with "And if you go …" through "… cried Mrs. Zuckerman."). Spelling, punctuation, and capitalization should be perfect.

____

____

____

____

____

____

____

____

____

Reading Notes

beano booth a forerunner of the game Bingo, using beans as markers
schemer a planner of a secret plot
grandstand the main seating area of a stadium

Vocabulary

1. Templeton's **keen** nose detected many fine smells in the air. ______
2. Templeton's keen nose **detected** many fine smells in the air. ______
3. "Well, I hope you're satisfied," **sneered** the rat. ______
4. He **vanished** into the shadows. ______
5. I will show you my **masterpiece**. ______

Comprehension Questions

1. What does Charlotte say about the web she is preparing? ______
2. What is the last word Charlotte weaves into her web? Why is it a perfect choice? ______
3. What three things does Charlotte do at the fair that are unusual? ______
4. Refer to the second quotation. What sights and sounds does Charlotte say will show that morning has come? ______

Quotations

The grownups climbed slowly into the truck and Wilbur heard the engine start and then heard the truck moving away in low speed. He would have felt lonely and homesick, had Charlotte not been with him. He never felt lonely when she was near.

"I'll tell you in the morning," she said. "When the first light comes into the sky and the sparrows stir and the cows rattle their chains, when the rooster crows and the stars fade, when early cars whisper along the highway, you look up here and I'll show you something. I will show you my masterpiece."

Discussion Questions

1. Find Dr. Dorian's prediction about Fern in Chapter 14. In what way does it come true in this chapter?
2. Consider the old sheep's prediction of the fair in Chapter 16. Compare the prediction to Templeton's experience in this chapter. Look for specific examples.

Enrichment

Character Pyramids - Wilbur and Charlotte: Fill in the pyramids below using one descriptive word in each blank to answer the corresponding statements.

Wilbur	Charlotte
__________	__________

one word telling how they react to the news of Wilbur's death

Wilbur	Charlotte
_______ _______	_______ _______

two words relating their attitude about humans

Wilbur	Charlotte
_____ _____ _____	_____ _____ _____

three words revealing the kind of friend they are

Wilbur	Charlotte
____ ____ ____ ____	____ ____ ____ ____

four words describing their personality

Reading Notes

nifty	slang expression for "excellent" or "fine"
magnum opus	Latin phrase meaning "great work"
acute attack of indigestion	severe case of abdominal pain due to overeating

Vocabulary

1. I don't feel good at all. I think I'm **languishing**. ______
2. people would pass by … **marveling** at the miracle. ______
3. he said in a **husky** voice. ______
4. What feasting and **carousing**! ______
5. A real **gorge**! I must have eaten the remains of thirty lunches. ______

Comprehension Questions

1. Describe Charlotte's egg sac. Why does she call it her *magnum opus*? ______
2. Describe the decline in Charlotte's behavior. ______
3. What bad news does Templeton share after his night of carousing? ______
4. What is Wilbur's response to Templeton's pronouncement of his coming death in this chapter? How is his reaction different than in previous chapters? ______
5. Why are the Zuckermans and Arables so joyful despite Avery's news? ______

Quotations

Charlotte's web never looked more beautiful than it looked this morning. Each strand held dozens of bright drops of early morning dew. The light from the east struck it and made it all plain and clear. it was a perfect piece of designing and building.

Up overhead, in the shadows of the ceiling, Charlotte crouched unseen, her front legs encircling her egg sac. Her heart was not beating as strongly as usual and she felt weary and old, but she was sure at last that she had saved Wilbur's life, and she felt peaceful and contented.

Discussion Questions

1. Where in *Charlotte's Web* have you seen similar imagery as in the first paragraph of this chapter? Why do you think the author chose to repeat this imagery?
2. *At the beginning of the book, Wilbur was worried about his future and focused on his own problems. How does this chapter show that Wilbur has learned to be a better friend to Charlotte? What elements of friendship does Charlotte continue to display?

Enrichment

Focus Passage - Dialogue: Recall that **dialogue** is used to show a character's exact words. Each time a different character begins to speak, a new paragraph is begun and indented.

Directions: Copy the paragraphs of dialogue on page 144 (beginning with "Are you awake …" through "… *magnum opus*."). Spelling, punctuation, and capitalization should be perfect.

Reading Notes

hour of triumph	a time of great victory
ladeez	exaggerated pronunciation for "ladies"
phenomenon	an extraordinary event

Vocabulary

1. said the loud speaker in a **pompous** voice. ______
2. we now present Mr. Homer L. Zuckerman's **distinguished** pig. ______
3. calling the attention of all and **sundry** to the fact ______
4. In the last **analysis**, we simply know ______
5. The pain **revived** Wilbur. ______

Comprehension Questions

1. What does Fern prefer to do rather than watch the award ceremony? ______
2. Why does Wilbur receive special recognition? ______
3. How does Wilbur react to the attention? ______
4. What does Avery do to get the crowd's attention? How do you know Avery enjoys being in the spotlight? ______

Quotations

"Note the general radiance of this animal! Then remember the day when the word 'radiant' appeared clearly on the web. Whence came this mysterious writing? Not from the spider, we can rest assured of that. Spiders are very clever at weaving their webs, but needless to say spiders cannot write."

Who said this? ______________________ On what occasion? ______________________

A great feeling of happiness swept over the Zuckermans and the Arables. This was the greatest moment in Mr. Zuckerman's life. It is deeply satisfying to win a prize in front of a lot of people.

Discussion Questions

1. *This chapter is titled "The Hour of Triumph." To whose triumph is the author referring?
2. What was Templeton's reason for biting Wilbur's tail?
3. Describe the scene after the photographer takes pictures of the event.

Enrichment

Dictation: Listen carefully as your teacher reads the paragraphs of dialogue on page 156 (beginning with "Can't you see I'm busy …" through "… don't point."). During the reading, write down what you hear. Then go back and make any necessary corrections in spelling, punctuation, or capitalization. When you are finished, compare your paragraph to the book and circle any errors.

REMEMBER! Indent and begin a new paragraph each time a different character begins to speak.

____

____

____

____

____

____

____

____

____

____

Reading Notes

monkeyshine a playful trick
wisecrack a short, witty joke poking fun at someone

Vocabulary

1. Your future is **assured**. ______
2. I thought you were cruel and **bloodthirsty**! ______
3. I was trying to lift up my life a **trifle**. ______
4. And I thank you for your generous **sentiments**. ______
5. Great sobs **racked** his body. ______
6. He heaved and grunted with **desolation**. ______

Comprehension Questions

1. How has Wilbur lifted up Charlotte's life a trifle? ______
2. What has Wilbur learned from Charlotte? ______
3. What is Templeton's role in Wilbur's plan? How does Wilbur convince him to help? ______
4. How does Wilbur transport the egg sac? Why is he so confident in this method? ______

Quotations

"Your success in the ring this morning was, to a small degree, ***my*** *success. Your future is assured. You will live, secure and safe, Wilbur. Nothing can harm you now."*

Who said this? ______________________________

But as he was being shoved into the crate, he looked up at Charlotte and gave her a wink. She knew he was saying good-bye in the only way he could. And she knew her children were safe.

Discussion Questions

1. *How has Templeton contributed to saving Wilbur's life? What is his attitude about helping?
2. *Describe the last moments Charlotte and Wilbur spend together.
3. *Reread the last paragraph of the chapter. What sad event occurs? How does the description of the activities at the fair grounds affect the mood of the paragraph?

Enrichment

Quotation Review: How good is your memory? Supply the name of the speaker for each quotation below. The quotations are taken from Chapters 16-21.

1. "A fair is a rat's paradise. Everybody spills food at a fair." ______________________________
2. "I think I'm going to faint." ______________________________
3. "I am going to give that pig a buttermilk bath." ______________________________
4. "What did you think I was, a spring chicken?" ______________________________
5. "I don't feel good at all. I think I'm languishing, to tell you the truth." ______________________________
6. "I must have eaten the remains of thirty lunches." ______________________________
7. "Henry invited me to go on the Ferris wheel again …" ______________________________
8. "You asked for water." ______________________________
9. "Humble, now isn't that just the word for Wilbur." ______________________________
10. "Look at this! This pig has won first prize already." ______________________________

Reading Notes

lee	the side of an object that is sheltered from the wind
Aranea	Latin word for "spider"
garrulous	given to excessive, rambling talk; tiresomely talkative
in a class by herself	a category of her own; no one could match her

Vocabulary

1. "The most fun there is," **retorted** Fern, "is when the Ferris wheel stops …" ____________________
2. whenever he found a **trinket** or a keepsake he carried it home ____________________
3. in **shrill** chorus, came the voices of … little frogs.____________________
4. We're leaving here on the warm **updraft**. ____________________
5. You have chosen a **hallowed** doorway ____________________
6. And many more happy, **tranquil** days followed. ____________________

Comprehension Questions

1. Describe the barn upon Wilbur's return. ____________________

____

____

____

2. How does Wilbur prepare for the birth of Charlotte's children? ____________________

____

____

3. What is Wilbur's reaction when the baby spiders are born? ____________________

____

____

____

4. Why is Wilbur so sad several days after Charlotte's children are born? ____________________

____

____

Quotations

Mr. Zuckerman took fine care of Wilbur all the rest of his days, and the pig was often visited by friends and admirers, for nobody ever forgot the year of his triumph and the miracle of the web.

Wilbur never forgot Charlotte. Although he loved her children and grandchildren dearly, none of the new spiders ever quite took her place in his heart. She was in a class by herself. It is not often that someone comes along who is a true friend and a good writer. Charlotte was both.

Discussion Questions

1. What seasonal changes occur on the farm in the winter and in the early spring?
2. *How does Wilbur's treatment of the baby spiders reflect character qualities he learned from Charlotte?
3. *Describe the changes that have occurred in Wilbur since the beginning of the book.

Enrichment

Composition: In your own words write a paragraph (3-5 sentences) describing your favorite character from *Charlotte's Web*. Include details about the character's appearance and personality, and explain *why* you like this character. When you are finished writing, correct any errors in spelling, punctuation, and capitalization.

Elements of Literature

Write sentences about the story.

Character

Character means <u>who</u> is in the story.

1. Write one sentence describing a change in Wilbur. ______________________________

   ____

2. Write one sentence describing a change in Charlotte. ____________________________

   ____

Setting

Setting means the <u>time</u> and <u>place</u> in which the story happens.

1. Write two sentences describing the County Fair. ________________________________

   ____

   ____

   ____

   ____

Plot

Plot means <u>action</u> or <u>what happens</u> in the story.

Directions: Sequence the events in order. Then, copy them in order onto the following page. Each event should be written below a separate box. Finally, illustrate each event in the box.

Events:

_____ Charlotte meets Wilbur's competition.

_____ Charlotte reveals her *magnum opus.*

_____ Charlotte's babies are born.

_____ Before leaving the farm, Wilbur gets a buttermilk bath.

_____ Templeton supplies the final web word.

_____ Wilbur faints while receiving his award.

Vocabulary

Write the letter of the vocabulary word on the line in front of its definition.

1. _______ greatest work	a. shrill
2. _______ high-pitched noise	b. listless
3. _______ struggle	c. keen
4. _______ growing weak	d. husky
5. _______ exceed; go beyond	e. gorge
6. _______ tiredly	f. trifle
7. _______ loneliness	g. revive
8. _______ full of exaggerated pride	h. wearily
9. _______ replied	i. sentiments
10. _______ sharp; highly developed	j. languishing
11. _______ spoke in a scornful manner	k. surpass
12. _______ restore to consciousness	l. masterpiece
13. _______ statements based on emotions	m. pompous
14. _______ hoarse	n. retorted
15. _______ to move upward	o. tussle
16. _______ special	p. desolation
17. _______ a binge of overeating	q. sneered
18. _______ disappeared	r. vanished
19. _______ small degree	s. ascend
20. _______ tired; no energy	t. distinguished

Short Answer

Answer the following questions in complete sentences.

1. What is the last word Charlotte weaves into her web, and why is it a perfect choice? ____________

2. Describe Charlotte's egg sac. Why does she call it her *magnum opus?* ____________

3. How do Charlotte and Wilbur spend their last moments together? ____________

4. How does Wilbur prepare for the birth of Charlotte's children? ____________

5. Describe two changes that have occurred in Wilbur since the beginning of the book. ____________

Vocabulary Crossword

Use your vocabulary knowledge from reading *Charlotte's Web* to complete the following crossword:

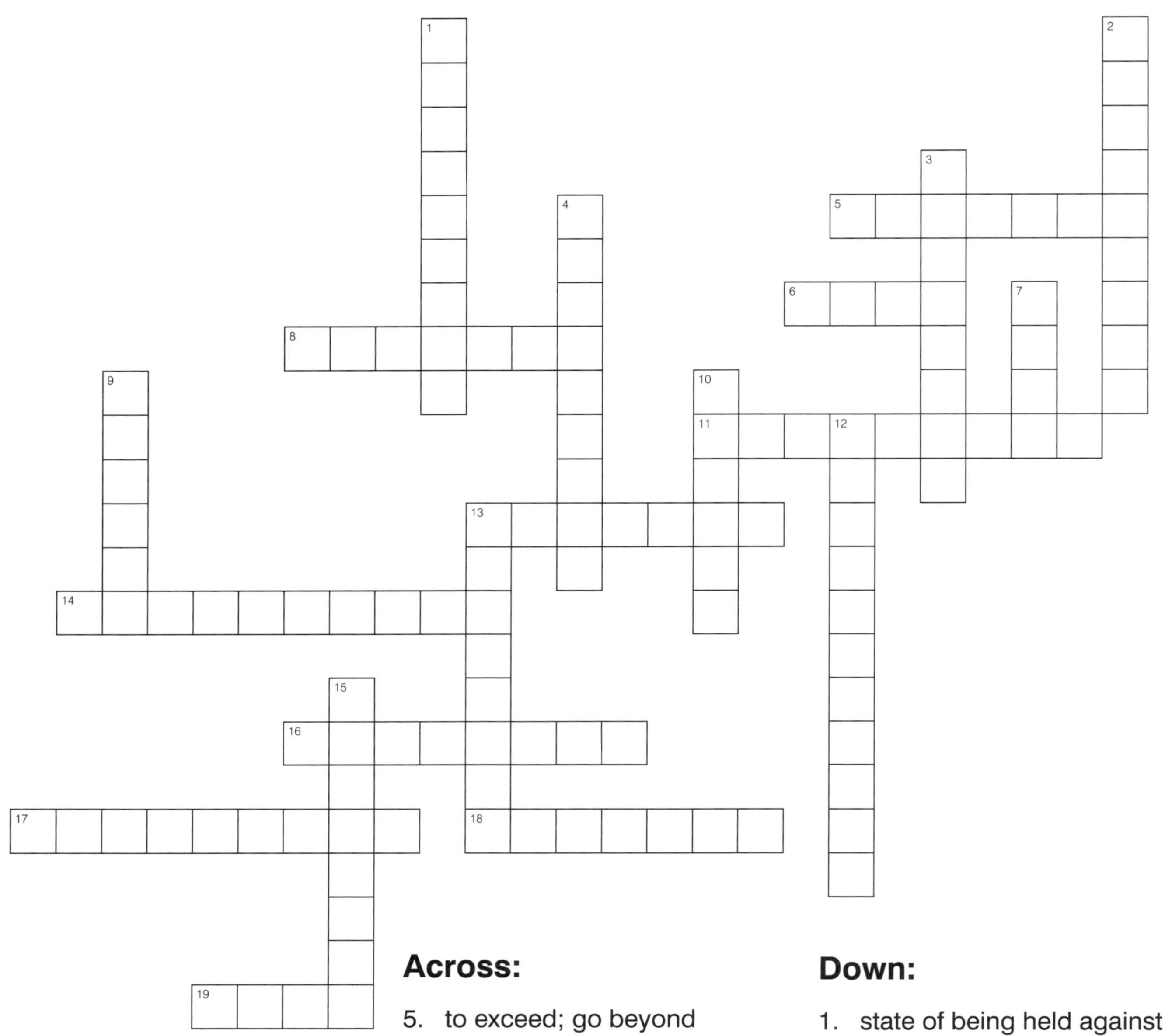

Across:

5. to exceed; go beyond
6. smallest of the litter
8. one who habitually overeats
11. gathering, calling up
13. strongly disliked
14. statements based on emotions
16. trembled
17. adaptable; can adjust easily
18. seriously; firmly
19. to look at steadily

Down:

1. state of being held against your will
2. endless; continuous
3. squirming
4. main; primary
7. sharp; highly developed
9. to restore to consciousness
10. to move upward
12. greatest work
13. tired; no energy
15. easily deceived

Word Bank

runt	sternly
gaze	incessant
captivity	versatile
glutton	surpass
loathed	ascend
summoning	listless
gullible	keen
principal	masterpiece
quivered	revive
writhing	sentiments

Character Identification

Using the name bank, match each name to a description and write the name on the line.

Mr. Arable	**Mrs. Zuckerman**	**Fern**	**Lurvy**	**Charlotte**
Wilbur	**Templeton**	**goose**	**old sheep**	**Avery**

1. ______________________ thought he was too young for freedom
2. ______________________ convinced Templeton that the fair is a rat's paradise
3. ______________________ was a glutton, but not a merrymaker
4. ______________________ believed people are gullible
5. ______________________ only distributed pigs to early risers
6. ______________________ was impressed with the stories of Charlotte's cousins
7. ______________________ built a crate for Wilbur
8. ______________________ believed that the spider was extraordinary, not the pig
9. ______________________ advised Wilbur during his escape
10. ______________________ loved lots of attention and performed to get more of it

Who Said That?

Write the name of the speaker on the line in front of each quotation.

1. ______________________ "No-no-no … It's the old pail trick, Wilbur. Don't fall for it!"
2. ______________________ "Pigs mean less than nothing to me."
3. ______________________ "Humble, now isn't that just the word for Wilbur."
4. ______________________ "Look at this! This pig has won first prize already."
5. ______________________ "But it's unfair … The pig couldn't help being born small, could it?"
6. ______________________ "I think I'm going to faint."
7. ______________________ "You asked for water."
8. ______________________ "I don't feel good at all. I think I'm languishing, to tell you the truth."
9. ______________________ "they're fattening you up because they're going to kill you"
10. ______________________ "I must have eaten the remains of thirty lunches."

Multiple Choice

Choose the **best** answer for each question.

1. How is Templeton convinced to get words from the dump?
   a. The old sheep points out that saving Wilbur means he will always have his leftover food to eat.
   b. Templeton is finally convinced that it won't take much extra time or effort since he makes regular trips to the dump anyway.
   c. The goose offers him another "dud" egg in the future if he will help Wilbur now.

2. What bad news is spreading in the barnyard?
   a. Fern can't visit Wilbur any more.
   b. Wilbur is going to be killed at Christmastime.
   c. Templeton has captured a baby goose.

3. Why does Charlotte say she cannot go to the fair with Wilbur?
   a. Nature says it is time to lay her eggs and she cannot delay it, not even for Wilbur.
   b. She wants Wilbur to gain confidence by going alone and succeeding without further help.
   c. She is confident her plan is working well and Wilbur no longer needs her help.

4. On what attribute does Charlotte rely to help her solve problems?
   a. She relies on her willingness to work hard.
   b. She depends on her intelligence; her ability to think of good ideas.
   c. She depends on her ability to wait patiently.

5. How does Fern pamper Wilbur? **Both** must be true!
   a. She gives him candy and lets him wade in the water.
   b. She takes him for rides and lets him sleep in her bed.
   c. She takes him for rides and lets him wade in the mud.

6. What advice does the old sheep give Wilbur before he is crated for the fair?
   a. He tells Wilbur to struggle as the men try to put him into the crate.
   b. He tells Wilbur to be sure to eat plenty of food before leaving because he may not get fed again until late in the evening.
   c. He tells Wilbur to watch Charlotte carefully since she is so weak.

7. What does Charlotte do that Wilbur describes as "real thoughtful"?
   a. She gives her prey an anaesthetic before drinking their blood.
   b. She becomes his friend.
   c. She captures flies so they won't bother other animals.

8. What is Wilbur's response to Templeton's pronouncement of Uncle's prize and Wilbur's death?
   a. Wilbur remains fairly calm and changes the subject.
   b. Wilbur starts to cry and asks Charlotte to tell him what to do.
   c. Wilbur panics and yells that he does not want to die.

9. What changes does Charlotte begin to notice in herself while at the fair?
   a. She feels a lack of energy and is tired all the time.
   b. She becomes very hungry and anxious to make a new web.
   c. She suddenly feels tired and hungry all the time.

10. Why is Wilbur so sad several days after Charlotte's children are born?
   a. The baby spiders make web balloons and float away to find new homes.
   b. He is lonely and bored because Fern no longer comes to visit.
   c. He misses Charlotte and wants to share the excitement of their birth with her.

Paragraph: 3-5 sentences

In your own words write a paragraph describing your favorite character from *Charlotte's Web*. Include details about the character's appearance and personality. Also explain why you like this character. ___

____

____

____

____

____

____

____

____

____

Short Answer: Write a phrase or sentence for each question.

1. What does the word "arable" mean? Why is it a good name for a farm family? ________________

2. Choose one minor character from the book (Mrs. Zuckerman, Dr. Dorian, Lurvy) and describe this person's reaction to Charlotte's web. ________________

3. List three ways in which life on the Zuckerman farm changes as a result of Wilbur's fame. ________________

4. Name one specific action Templeton does to help Wilbur and describe how it displays his selfishness. ________________

5. Describe one specific character quality that Wilbur learns from Charlotte and later displays toward her children. ________________

6. What is the overall plot of *Charlotte's Web*? What is the one central problem in the book and how is it solved? ________________

Appendix

BIOGRAPHICAL SKETCH

Elwyn Brooks White (1899-1985), was born on July 11, in Mount Vernon, New York. His father was a piano manufacturer, and while the family was not wealthy, they lived comfortably. As a young man, he attended Cornell University, graduating in 1921.

After college, he was offered a teaching position in Minnesota which he turned down. He desired to become a writer and felt periodicals might suit him better. He became a reporter for the *Seattle Times*. This did not turn out to be a good fit for him and he left the position after about two years. He was then employed by an advertising agency as a production assistant and copywriter. During this time of his career he enjoyed the publication of his first poems.

In 1925 he published his first article in *The New Yorker* magazine, which eventually led to a position as contributing editor in 1927. He continued as editor there throughout the rest of his life. This was a major influential change in his career as *The New Yorker* from the time of its origin was one of the nation's most prestigious periodicals, featuring many writing celebrities of the time.

He married Katherine Sergeant, a fellow editor, in 1929. They eventually had one son. In the years that followed, he published various poems, essays, and essay collections, as well as continuing his periodical contributions to *The New Yorker* and *Harper's* magazine.

White entered the field of children's literature in 1945 with the publication of *Stuart Little*. Years later, in 1952, he again turned to children's literature with the publication of *Charlotte's Web,* his most well-known work in this genre. This is the story of the unique friendship between a runt pig and a common barn spider. It sets forth for children enduring examples of loyalty and self-sacrifice in friendship, as well as serving as a gentle lesson on the reality of death.

E. B. White is also known for his association with William S. Strunk, Jr., a professor at Cornell during the years White was a student there. He took a course from Strunk, using a small book Strunk had written for the purpose. White later edited, revised, and contributed a chapter to this book, *The Elements of Style,* which was well received and became a widely used college text in subsequent years.

Around this time he began to receive multiple honors for his writing. These include the Laura Ingalls Wilder Medal for his children's books in 1970 and the National Medal for Literature in 1971. He was also elected to the American Academy of Arts and Letters in 1973. Still more publishing successes followed, including the children's book, *The Trumpet of the Swan,* in 1970 and various collections of his letters, essays, poems, and sketches.

E. B. White has been a great influence in the field of literature. His essays have served as models for generations of writers, and *the New Yorker*, considered by critics of his time to be a model of elegant, simple non-fiction, owes no small debt to White for its quality reputation.

SPIDERS

Spiders are a member of the arachnid family, along with scorpions, mites, and ticks. They vary greatly in appearance; some are dull shades of gray or brown, others may be brilliant colors of red, yellow, or orange. Most spiders have a life span of two to three years.

All arachnid bodies consist of two parts—the head and the abdomen. They never have antennae or wings, but they do have eight jointed legs which are covered with hair that is sensitive to movement and used to help them grip the web. All spiders have fangs which produce venom for killing prey, and six to twelve eyes, though most have poor vision and rely on their ability to sense movement with their body hairs. A spider also has three or four pairs of spinnerets which produce silk. Liquid silk from inside the spider's body is sent out through these spinnerets to form many fine thin strands of thread which harden as they are exposed to the air and pulled on by the spider. Several strands joined together make up the sticky, durable lines of silk used to spin its web.

Not all spiders weave webs, but for those that do, the web serves as its means to capture prey for food. After the sticky web fibers have either attracted or captured its victim, the spider quickly approaches and wraps the prey with silk, immobilizing it. Since a spider cannot eat solid food, it must break it down before it is actually eaten. When the spider's fangs enter its prey, they inject poison and digestive juices into it. As these juices dissolve the body tissues, the spider simply drinks the resulting fluids out of its victim, leaving it to look undamaged on the outside. It later discards the inedible remains from the web.

Most spiders lay their eggs in a silk sac. Some carry this sac with them, others attach it to a web and camouflage it until the "spiderlings" are born. Since spiders do not have wings to carry them long distances, they must rely on different techniques to allow them to leave their original nest and form new homes. Many species use their silk threads as a sail with which to launch themselves into the wind to be carried to a new location. Others use "ballooning" which also relies on the wind; the spiderling stands in an exposed area, perhaps on the end of a branch, and lets out a droplet of silk. This drop is expanded and pulled by the wind, carrying the spider aloft, sometimes hundreds of miles away.

There are many different kinds of spiders. Each type has unique characteristics, life cycle, diet and style of web or home. Though varied in nature, most spiders are not harmful to people. Rather, they serve the important purpose of controlling harmful or destructive insects. The beauty and diversity displayed throughout the species is a vibrant reminder of God's awe-inspiring creativity.

TO A FRIEND

by Grace Stricker Dawson

You entered my life in a casual way,
  And saw at a glance what I needed;
There were others who passed me or met me each day,
  But never a one of them heeded.
Perhaps you were thinking of other folks more,
  Or chance simply seemed to decree it;
I know there were many such chances before,
  But the others—well, they didn't see it.

You said just the thing that I wished you would say,
  And you made me believe that you meant it;
I held up my head in the old gallant way,
  And resolved you should never repent it.
There are times when encouragement means such a lot,
  And a word is enough to convey it;
There were others who could have, as easy as not—
  But, just the same, they didn't say it.

There may have been someone who could have done more
  To help me along, though I doubt it;
What I needed was cheering, and always before
  They had let me plod onward without it.
You helped to refashion the dream of my heart,
  And made me turn eagerly to it;
There were others who might have (I question that part)—
  But, after all, they didn't do it!

THE SPIDER AND THE FLY

by Mary Howitt

"Will you walk into my parlour?" said the Spider to the Fly,
"'Tis the prettiest little parlour that ever you did spy;
The way into my parlour is up a winding stair,
And I've a many curious things to show when you are there."
"Oh no, no," said the little Fly, "to ask me is in vain,
For who goes up your winding stair can ne'er come down again."

"I'm sure you must be weary, dear, with soaring up so high;
Will you rest upon my little bed?" said the Spider to the Fly.
"There are pretty curtains drawn around; the sheets are fine and thin,
And if you like to rest awhile, I'll snugly tuck you in!"
"Oh no, no," said the little Fly, "for I've often heard it said,
They never, never wake again, who sleep upon your bed!"

Said the cunning Spider to the Fly, "Dear friend what can I do,
To prove the warm affection I've always felt for you?
I have within my pantry, good store of all that's nice;
I'm sure you're very welcome—will you please to take a slice?"
"Oh no, no," said the little Fly, "kind sir, that cannot be,
I've heard what's in your pantry, and I do not wish to see!"

"Sweet creature!" said the Spider, "you're witty and you're wise,
How handsome are your gauzy wings, how brilliant are your eyes!
I've a little looking-glass upon my parlour shelf,
If you'll step in one moment, dear, you shall behold yourself."
"I thank you, gentle sir," she said, "for what you're pleased to say,
And bidding you good morning now, I'll call another day."

The Spider turned him round about, and went into his den,
For well he knew the silly Fly would soon come back again:
So he wove a subtle web, in a little corner sly,
And set his table ready, to dine upon the Fly.
Then he came out to his door again, and merrily did sing,
"Come hither, hither, pretty Fly, with the pearl and silver wing;
Your robes are green and purple—there's a crest upon your head;
Your eyes are like the diamond bright, but mine are dull as lead!"

Alas, alas! how very soon this silly little Fly,
Hearing his wily, flattering words, came slowly flitting by;
With buzzing wings she hung aloft, then near and nearer drew,
Thinking only of her brilliant eyes, and green and purple hue—
Thinking only of her crested head—poor foolish thing! At last,
Up jumped the cunning Spider, and fiercely held her fast.
He dragged her up his winding stair, into his dismal den,
Within his little parlour—but she ne'er came out again!

And now, dear little children, who may this story read,
To idle, silly, flattering words, I pray you ne'er give heed:
Unto an evil counselor, close heart and ear and eye,
And take a lesson from this tale, of the Spider and the Fly.

THE SPIDER'S WEB

(A Natural History)

by E. B. White

The spider, dropping down from twig,
Unfolds a plan of her devising,
A thin premeditated rig
To use in rising.

And all that journey down through space,
In cool descent and loyal hearted,
She spins a ladder to the place
From where she started.

Thus I, gone forth as spiders do
In spider's web a truth discerning,
Attach one silken thread to you
For my returning.

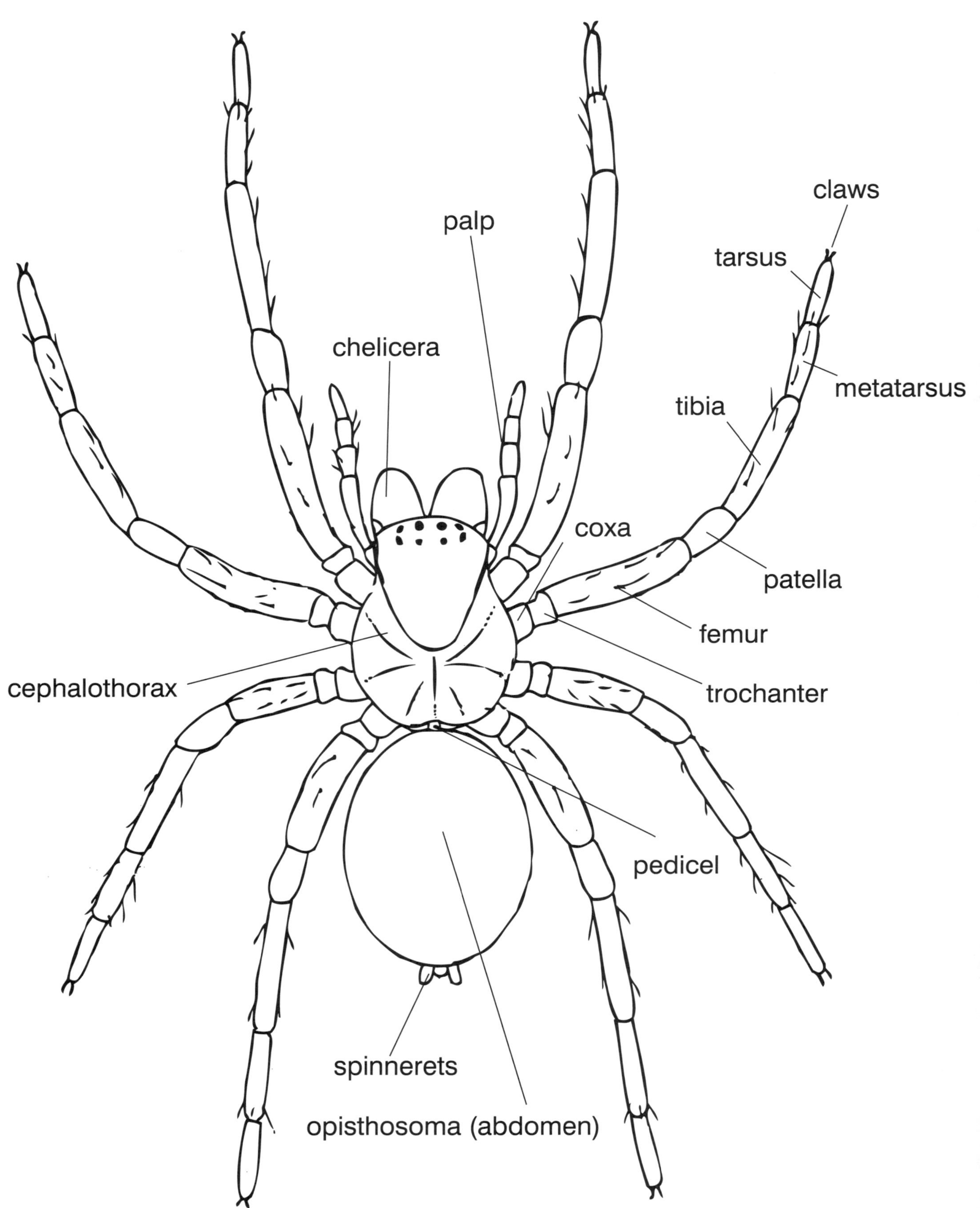
claws
palp
tarsus
chelicera
metatarsus
tibia
coxa
patella
femur
cephalothorax
trochanter
pedicel
spinnerets
opisthosoma (abdomen)